Greece & Rome

NEW SURVEYS IN THE CLASSICS No. 8

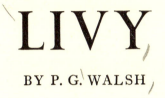

LIVY

BY P. G. WALSH

OXFORD

AT THE CLARENDON PRESS

1974

Oxford University Press, Ely House, London W. 1

GLASGOW NEW YORK TORONTO MELBOURNE WELLINGTON
CAPE TOWN IBADAN NAIROBI DAR ES SALAAM LUSAKA ADDIS ABABA
DELHI BOMBAY CALCUTTA MADRAS KARACHI LAHORE DACCA
KUALA LUMPUR SINGAPORE HONG KONG TOKYO

*Printed in Great Britain
at the University Press, Oxford
by Vivian Ridler
Printer to the University*

INTRODUCTION

IN this *libellus* I have not attempted to offer a systematic bibliography, which the reader may seek elsewhere,[1] but a general assessment of Livy as historian and literary artist as he appears to students of our generation. For this reason most of the work cited in support is of fairly recent date. But the image by which medieval thinkers expressed their debt to the philosophers and poets of Greece and Rome has its application here; we are 'dwarfs standing on the shoulders of giants',[2] and the modern studies quoted here will guide interested readers back to the scholars of earlier generations and their fundamental contributions.

When I published a general study of Livy a dozen years ago,[3] it was fair to complain of neglect of the historian by scholars writing in English. The following pages show how the situation is changing substantially. A central figure in this Livian revival is A. H. McDonald, whose Cambridge teaching has directly guided many, and whose researches on the text, thought, and style of the historian have stimulated contributions from a wider circle. His chapter 'The Roman Historians' in *Fifty Years of Classical Scholarship*[4] is characteristic for its breadth of vision; his synoptic view of Livy with predecessors and successors is an ideal starting-point for deeper study of the historian. Other general contributions in English may be found in recent surveys of ancient historians, and in a new collection of essays edited by T. A. Dorey.[5] These may be set beside the well-known general surveys in Italian, German, and French, and beside the recent *Wege der Forschung* volume.[6] The editor of that volume, Erich Burck, may fairly be called

[1] Apart from the yearly lists in *L'Année Philologique*, there is the useful survey of K. Gries, 'Livian Scholarship since 1940', *CW* liii (1959–60), 33 ff., 69 ff., and for earlier work, N. I. Herescu, *Bibliographie de la littérature latine* (Paris, 1943), 221 ff., and (for 1920–32) R. Rau in Bursian's *Jahresberichte* ccxlii (1934), 75 ff. A comprehensive bibliography of Livy is sorely needed.

[2] John of Salisbury, *Metalogicon* iii. 4.

[3] *Livy, his Historical Aims and Methods* (Cambridge, 1961). The bibliography contains older books and articles not mentioned here.

[4] Ed. Platnauer (Oxford, 1954); the revised edition, *Fifty Years and Twelve* (1968), contains additional bibliography.

[5] See especially M. Grant, *The Ancient Historians* (London, 1970), ch. 14; also S. Usher, *The Historians of Greece and Rome* (London, 1969), ch. 6; T. A. Dorey ed., *Latin Historians* (London, 1966), has a chapter on Livy by the present writer. Dorey is also the editor of the essays in *Livy* (London, 1971).

[6] See above all the Introduction to the Budé Livy i by J. Bayet, and the *Einleitung* in Weissenborn–Müller (Appendix, A11 and B6). Also P. Zancan, *Tito Livio saggio storico* (Milan, 1940); H. Bornecque, *Tite-Live* (Paris, 1933), and L. Catin, *En lisant*

the *doyen* of this generation of Livian scholars; the bibliography in the following pages will reveal the extent of his own contributions and of the researches of his pupils at Kiel.

Tite-Live (Paris, 1944); E. Burck ed., *Wege zu Livius* (Darmstadt, 1967). H. Taine, *Essai sur Tite-Live*[5] (Paris, 1888), deserves mention here *pietatis causa*.

I. THE AUGUSTAN HISTORIAN

DURING the past forty years the dominant preoccupation of scholars writing on Livy has been the relationship between the historian and the emperor Augustus, and its effects on the *Ab Urbe Condita*. Tacitus' testimony that the two were on friendly terms, and Suetonius' revelation that Livy found time to encourage the historical studies of the future emperor Claudius,[1] appeared to have ominous overtones to scholars writing against the political backcloth of Nazi Germany and Fascist Italy. Though the subject had not been wholly ignored previously,[2] the success of the German cultural propaganda-machine[3] stimulated a spate of approving or critical treatments. While some were hailing Livy as the historian whose work signalled and glorified the new order,[4] others following a similar interpretation were markedly scathing. 'With Livy we are far removed from the Thucydidean sense of history as a diligent and meticulous search for truth. ... What Livy offers us is rather an unabashed tract for the times; the Augustan version, in fact, of Plato's noble lie. And if this involves an element of artistic distortion, such distortion is justified in view of the purpose to be served. ... That purpose may be described, in the vernacular, as an attempt to "sell" the Augustan system.'[5] And the most influential interpretation of the fall of the Republic to have appeared in this century, Sir Ronald Syme's *The Roman Revolution*, speaks of Augustan poetry and history being 'designed to work upon the upper and middle classes of a regenerated society ... The Emperor and his historian understood each other.'[6]

This view of Livy as propagandist for the regime is now happily out of favour. Syme himself, in a characteristically ambivalent yet stimulating paper, modifies his standpoint to visualize Livy as 'the last of the Republican writers', 'not a flatterer and a timeserver', yet one who in the early books obliquely approves the avowed monarchy of Augustus, and in the final, lost sections writes 'in joyful acceptance of

---

[1] Tac. *Ann.* iv. 34; Suet. *Claud.* xli. 1.

[2] See, for example, H. Dessau, 'Livius und Augustus', *Hermes* xli (1906), 142 ff.

[3] Many of my generation will recall the notorious name of A. Rosenberg in this connection; his doctrines of alleged Aryan superiority I recall being read to us at school by a classics master demonstrating the power of tendentious history.

[4] Cf. W. Aly, *Livius und Ennius* (Leipzig, 1936); G. Stübler, *Die Religiosität des Livius* (Stuttgart, 1941); more circumspectly, F. Klingner, *Römische Geisteswelt*[2] (München, 1961), 444 ff.

[5] C. N. Cochrane, *Christianity and Classical Culture* (Oxford, 1940), 98 f., 103.

[6] Ronald Syme, *The Roman Revolution* (Oxford, 1939), 317, 468.

the new order, in praise of the government and its achievements'.[1] That these judgements should not be accepted unequivocally is indicated by the fact that other scholars interpret the same evidence to reach very different conclusions. Thus H. Petersen concludes after analysis of passages in the first book that Livy, so far from recommending Augustus' monarchy, 'intended to warn his contemporaries, especially Augustus . . . his message being: Romans will not tolerate an unmitigated monarchy.' And H. J. Mette has attempted to demonstrate that Livy's final books were critical of the Augustan principate.[2]

In this welter of speculation, which extends to the dates of composition of the first and final books,[3] certain key factors should be noted. (1) When we are told in Tacitus that Livy was pro-Pompeian, and generous in his praise of Brutus and Cassius, this is put forward as evidence of his independence of interpretation.[4] (2) The Preface is markedly pessimistic about the immediate prospect of moral resurgence at Rome, so that for Livy the contemplation of earlier centuries is an anodyne.[5] (3) The political attitudes reflected in Livy's account of the conflict of the orders suggest that he prescribes a return to the uncorrupted senatorial government of the Republic, and abhors autocracy.[6] (4) The actual references to Augustus in the *Ab Urbe Condita* are respectful but not adulatory or apologetic.[7] In short, Livy does not consciously lend his services as historian to the consolidation of the Augustan regime.

It is of course possible to argue that the historian's exhortation to a return to traditional Roman standards of political concord and private morality initially suited 'the Restorer of the Republic' well enough. An interpretation influential especially amongst Italian scholars suggests

[1] Ronald Syme, 'Livy and Augustus', *HSCP* lxiv (1959), 71, 53, 47, 75.

[2] Hans Petersen, 'Livy and Augustus', *TAPA* xcii (1961), 440 ff.; H. J. Mette, 'Livius und Augustus', *Gymn.* lxviii (1961), 278 ff. = *Wege zu Livius*, 156 ff., on which see R. M. Ogilvie, *Gnomon* xl (1968), 509 ff.

[3] If these dates could be established, they would be important in assessing the effect of Augustus' influence on the *Ab Urbe Condita*. Most scholars believe that the first pentad was finished by 27 B.C., and that Augustus' discovery of the linen corslet of Cossus necessitated a revision of the comments at iv. 20 about that time. See J. Bayet, Budé Livy I. xvii f., arguing for initial publication in 31–29 and revision in 27–5; R. Syme (p. 6 n. 1) and T. J. Luce, *TAPA* lxxi (1965), 209 ff., suggest the revision was made about 27. E. Mensching, *M.H.* xxiv (1967), 12 ff., suggests a first edition in the early 20s and a revision about 24. These assessments virtually exclude the possibility that Augustus could personally have influenced Livy's account of early history. At the other end, the Periocha of Book CXXI suggests that the publication of the book was withheld till after Augustus' death, and the assumption is justifiable that some of the content of CXXI–CXLII was unflattering to Augustus. See Ogilvie, *A Commentary on Livy Books I–V* (Oxford, 1965), 3, and Luce's good article cited above.

[4] Tac. *Ann.* iv. 34.   [5] *Praef.* 5 and 9.

[6] e.g. ii. 1. 1, 9. 7 f., 15. 2 ff., iii. 39. 8, vi. 20. 5 f. See Walsh, 'Livy and Augustus', *PACA* iv (1961), 8 ff.

[7] See Mensching (p. 6 n. 3), 12 ff., 25.

that, though sturdily independent of Augustus, Livy reflects the aspirations of the Italian bourgeoisie, who united with the nobility under the banner of *libertas* to block social revolution and thus to establish the principate.[1] It should be noted that even if this political interpretation is accepted, no charge of collusion is involved. Livy's ideal of Roman government was a far cry from the autocracy eventually transmitted by Augustus to Tiberius.

Livy's political ideas are in fact more fruitfully studied against national traditions[2] than against Augustus' political aspirations. The historian must obviously have responded to the prospect of a more stable and harmonious political life with the onset of the *pax Augusta*, and to this extent it is relevant to tease out of his work the political, social, and religious emphases which echo contemporary preoccupations.[3] But these ideas in no sense militate against Republican values; Livy is the Republican traditionalist *par excellence*.

[1] See M. Mazza, *Storia e ideologia in Livio* (Catania, 1966), ch. 7, where the views of S. Mazzarino and A. la Penna are closely reflected.

[2] See H. Hoch, *Die Darstellung der politischen Sendung Roms bei Livius* (Frankfurt, 1951); P. Fraccaro, 'Livio e Roma', *Opuscula* i (Pavia, 1956), 81 ff.

[3] Cf. E. Burck, 'Livius als augusteischer Historiker', *Die Welt als Geschichte* i (1935), 448 ff. = *Wege zu Livius*, 96 ff.; M. A. Levi, 'Tito Livio e gli ideali augustei', *PP* iv (1949), 15 ff.

II. LIVY AS THE HISTORIAN OF ROME

A. *The Over-all Interpretation: Structure and Preface*

A RECURRENT feature of earlier research into Livy's work has been the assumption, based on the highly rhetorical exordium to the fourth decade[1] and also on the difficulty of demonstrating clear principles of structural division, that there is no over-all plan to lend coherence to his interpretation of the history of the Republic. The present climate of Latin literary studies demands fresh scrutiny of this assumption; recent studies of other genres of Augustan literature have underlined the almost obsessive attention paid to artistic structure. Moreover, Livy's extant books reveal how much care he devoted to the patterning of events by decades and pentads. There is no dispute that I–V form a unit;[2] VI–XV are devoted to the period fom the Gallic crisis to the outbreak of the Punic Wars;[3] XVI–XX cover the First Punic War and its aftermath, XXI–XXX the Second Punic War (with demonstrably careful internal structuring),[4] XXXI–XXXV the Second Macedonian War, XXXVI–XL the wars with Antiochus and Aetolia, and XLI–XLV the Third Macedonian War.[5] P. Jal has recently edited the first books of the fifth decade, and he concludes that the decade as a whole forms one unit, its scope being the years 178–148 B.C. and its theme the death-throes of an independent Macedonia.[6]

The thesis that in the subsequent lost books such an artistic division by pentads and decades collapses has been argued by scholars from Weissenborn and Nissen to Bayet and Syme.[7] Stadter's recent notable article refutes this view, and indicates an acceptable solution.[1] The first fifty books mark the acquisition of empire, and are therefore divided according to *external* criteria (I–XV domination of Italy, XVI–XXX

---

[1] xxxi. 1. 5: 'iam provideo animo, velut qui proximis litori vadis inducti mare pedibus ingrediuntur, quidquid progredior in vastiorem me altitudinem ac velut profundum invehi, et crescere paene opus quod prima quaeque perficiendo minui videbatur.'

[2] See Ogilvie's *Commentary* (p. 6 n. 3), 30; and E. Burck, *Die Erzählungskunst des T. Livius* (Berlin, 1934; new impression with fresh Introduction, 1964).

[3] With a subdivision at the end of X at L. Papirius Cursor's significant victory over the Samnites in 293; see P. A. Stadter, 'The Structure of Livy's History', *Historia* xxi (1972), 294.

[4] See E. Burck in *Livy* (p. 3 n. 5), 22 f.

[5] See now F. W. Walbank in *Livy* (p. 3 n. 5), 48 f.

[6] Budé edn. of XLI–XLII (Paris, 1971), vii ff.

[7] Syme's comment is typical: 'If Livy began his work with decades in mind, they cracked and broke under pressure of the matter.'

[8] See above, p. 8 n. 3.

the first two Punic Wars, XXXI–L the subjugation of opposition in Macedonia, Greece, and Asia). But the principle of the subsequent division is *internal*, depicting the stages of the moral collapse which Livy outlines in his Preface. The turning-point in Book LI was naturally enough the fall of Carthage in 146; in this Livy follows Poseidonius, Sallust, and others. The Preface outlines three subsequent stages (here I extend Stadter's argument) which accord well with the division by decades.[1] So LI–LX treat the years from the fall of Carthage to the legislation of Gaius Gracchus in 123/2 (*labente paulatim disciplina*), LXI–LXX the thirty years between the revolutionary tribunates of Gaius Gracchus and Livius Drusus (*ut mores magis magisque lapsi sint*), and LXXI begins the description of the final disintegration (*tum ire coeperint praecipites*) with the commencement of the Social War.

This final stage of degeneration continues over the fifty books LXXI–CXX, and the principle of its subdivision into decades is crystal clear, for the units are structured round the careers of the dominant personalities. Marius is the central figure of the eighth decade, which covers the five years in which the revolutionary policies of the *populares* came to fruition; Livy closes LXXX with a memorable appreciation of their dead leader. The ninth decade, dominated by Sulla, takes in the eight years of the counter-revolution between his Athenian operations of 86 and his death in 78. The rise of Pompey is the central theme of the tenth decade, and culminates in the extraordinary powers he won in 66; the eleventh decade delineates his years of dominance up to the Greek campaign of 48 B.C. CXI–CXX take the reader on from the fall and death of Pompey to the murder of Cicero at the close of 43 B.C., the first pentad being devoted to the decisive engagements of the Civil War from Dyrrhachium to Munda. The death of Cicero and the formation of the second triumvirate mark for Livy the end of the story; when he planned his work in the thirties, his design may have extended only to CXX, and the last twenty-two books, which he is said to have held back until after Augustus' death,[2] may have been composed as an appendix devoted to contemporary events, like Polybius' final books.

This analysis of Livy's artistic division is no idle academic exercise. The annalistic historian, who was committed to a year-by-year survey of the multifarious events occurring within the imperial borders, could not easily select and shape incidents to a pattern of his own devising. The structuring by pentads and decades was Livy's chief method of indicating his historical interpretation. Following his immediate

[1] 'labente deinde paulatim disciplina velut desidentes primo mores . . . deinde ut magis magisque lapsi sint, tum ire coeperint praecipites.'
[2] See above, p. 6 n. 3.

predecessor Sallust,[1] he regarded the history of the Republic up to the fall of Carthage[2] as a period in which a healthy political and moral climate allowed the empire to be established and extended. The decline sets in with the absence of *metus hostilis* and the ensuing *otium;* the state is infected by the *furor* of Tiberius Gracchus' civic disturbances and by the *perniciosae leges* of his brother Gaius.[3] The moral malaise spreads to the governing class during 122–92 B.C. (LXI–LXX), as is evidenced by the venality of Roman senators and by the indiscipline of Roman commanders during the wars with Jugurtha and the Cimbri. The final stage, covering the entire half-century from 91 to 43 B.C., witnesses the corruption of the whole body politic.[4] Though Livy is more disposed to unequivocal condemnation of the Gracchi than is Sallust, and in general adopts a High Tory attitude towards the agitation of the *populares,* he criticizes the violence of Sulla's counter-revolution, described in the ninth decade, as strongly as he censures the revolutionary policies of Marius in the eighth. In this sense we are to visualize the historian making a manful effort to judge events and personalities *sine ira et studio,* to stand poised philosophically above the conflict whilst indicating his nostalgia for the senatorial government as it was maintained before 150 B.C.

Livy's general attitudes towards his theme are expounded in his eloquent Preface, on which M. Mazza has written a comprehensive monograph[5] which incorporates earlier work on the subject.[6] Mazza's candidly ideological interpretation, dismissing Livy's history as 'fantasia storica', may alienate some readers by political oversimplification but is none the less a valuable account of the Preface in the tradition of Greek and Roman prologues. Livy's is a more personal statement than

---

[1] Whereas Polybius and Calpurnius Piso saw perceptible moral decline in the 160s and 150s, for Sallust the period between 201 and 150 is marked by *optimis moribus* and *maxima concordia* (fr. 11M). See in general the fine study of D. C. Earl, *The Political Thought of Sallust* (Cambridge, 1961). But Livy does not single out the last fifty years as the high point of Republican manners as Sallust does.

[2] The fall of Carthage as the watershed in Livy's history is reflected in Florus i. 34, iii. 12; Orosius v. 1.

[3] Periochae 58–60 with their anti-Gracchan presentation thus signal Livy's divergence from the Sallustian thesis that both sides were guilty, but that the nobility having the greater power bore the greater responsibility.

[4] As the first stage was anticipated by Poseidonius, whose history began at 146 B.C., so the final stage was adapted from Sisenna, who began his work at 91 B.C.

[5] See p. 7 n. 1, and my review in *Gnomon* xxxix (1967), 783–6.

[6] Note especially H. Dessau, 'Die Vorrede des Livius', *Festschr. O. Hirschfeld* (Berlin, 1903), 461 ff.; L. Amundsen, 'Notes to the Preface of Livy', *SO* xxv (1947), 31 ff.; G. Funaioli, 'Il proemio alle storie di T. Livio', *St. Lett. Ant.* ii. 2 (1947), 47 ff.; L. Ferrero, 'Attualità e tradizione nella Praefatio liviana', *RFIC* xxvii (1949), 1 ff.; Walsh, 'Livy's Preface and the Distortion of History', *AJP* lxxvi (1955), 369 ff. See also T. Janson, *Latin Prose Prefaces* (Stockholm, 1964); Ogilvie, *Commentary*, 23 ff., with additional bibliography

any of his predecessors'. Engagingly modest in his apprehension at the mammoth task before him (§ 4), and candidly confessing to an escapist desire to quit by his studies the depressing contemporary scene (§ 5), he declares his passionate conviction that the earlier Republic possessed unique moral stature ('nulla umquam respublica nec maior nec sanctior' (§ 11)) and recommends emulation of its public and private virtues (§ 10). This is the voice of the non-political moralist, interested not so much in the techniques by which power is obtained and manipulated as in the deeper attributes of character possessed by the Roman leaders and their antagonists. In this sense Livy is less engaged in the harsh political realities than are Sallust and Tacitus, and his more philosophic vision is that of the detached academic.

Such detachment, it should be stressed, ran counter to the earlier tradition of historiography at Rome, in which history had been largely the preserve of political leaders, and was exploited both for national propaganda and to reinforce the political claims of groups within the state.[1] But Livy's immediate annalistic predecessors, Valerius Antias and Claudius Quadrigarius, were not active politicians; they are representative of a developing tradition of armchair composition, in which Livy emerges as the first major figure of such 'autonomous' historiography. The rules which he follows are those prescribed by Cicero.[2] Within the annalistic structure which affords the essential chronological clarity, events are described in the sequence of *consilia, acta, eventus;* these are not fabulous anecdotes or *deverticula amoena,* but the stuff of pragmatic history, military and political. The central concern is the achievement of leading men, whose careers and characters must be described. In them is embodied the didactic message which Livy preaches: *inde tibi tuaeque reipublicae quod imitere capias.*[3]

B. *Philosophical and Religious Ideas*

The influence of Cicero was not confined to historiographical theory; Livy showed himself a Ciceronian also in his philosophical preoccupations. It is unfortunate that his philosophical works have not survived, because they would have clarified the historian's fundamental attitudes towards the gods and the world. In default of Livy's own dialogues (Seneca's description of them suggests that some were directly philosophical and others both historical and philosophical),[4] it is useful to

---

[1] See E. Badian's chapter 'The Early Historians' in *Latin Historians* (p. 3 n. 5). R. Klein, *Königtum und Königszeit bei Cicero* (diss. Erlangen, 1962), demonstrates how historical evidence was still being manipulated in the final decades of the Republic.

[2] Cic. *De Or.* ii. 36 ff., 51 ff. See M. Rambaud, *Cicéron et l'histoire romaine* (Paris, 1953); E. Rawson, 'Cicero the Historian and Cicero the Antiquarian', *JRS* lxii (1972), 33 ff.

[3] *Praef.* 10.   [4] Seneca, *Ep.* 100. 9. See A. Engelbrecht, *WS* xxvi (1904), 62 ff.

examine how Cicero had attempted to accommodate Greek philosophical thinking to a framework of Roman traditional ideas.[1] It is important also in this respect to obtain a proper understanding of Roman piety.[2]

The interaction between Greek philosophy and Roman traditional theology lies at the root of Livy's ambivalence towards the gods and their role in the history of Roman man. On the one hand, he constantly underlines the central importance attached to religious observance by those earlier Romans whom he bids his contemporaries imitate, and he frequently depicts the disasters attending on *impietas*. On the other hand there are regular glimpses of the rationalizing mind at work, tacitly dissenting from traditional accounts of divine interventions in Rome's early years and scathingly condemning the religiosity and superstition prompted by allegedly divine signs and portents.

Inevitably this ambivalence has stimulated a wide divergence in assessments of Livy's philosophical and theological views. These are well summarized in an article by W. Liebeschuetz.[3] After reviewing the theories of Livy as agnostic, as orthodox believer, as rationalizing Stoic, his analysis of key-passages leads him to the conclusion that in Livy the 'awe and reverence induced by sacred objects or rites' co-exists with 'a rationalist outlook on the world'. We are back where we started, with the dichotomy between traditional religious observance and rationalizing philosophy. Some like Liebeschuetz must be content to leave it there, while others visualize Livy as a latter-day Cotta, or alternatively as a Balbus[4]—such differing interpretations resulting from varying assessments of Livy's philosophical preoccupations, and from the interpreters' own subjective insights.

Common to these views is the recognition that in Livy's eyes events are determined chiefly by human qualities.[5] It would be a misunderstanding to assume that this effectively excludes the religious dimension; here a study of the Ciceronian dialogues *De divinatione* and *De natura deorum* is especially rewarding for the notion of a universe effectively governed by an ethical determinism. Observance of the traditional virtues by Roman leaders makes for national and individual prosperity, and those who espouse the vices equally inevitably court disaster. There is no question of the imposition of an external *Diktat* by divini-

[1] See the excellent chapter of A. E. Douglas in Dorey ed., *Cicero* (London, 1964), and at greater length the brave book of H. A. K. Hunt, *The Humanism of Cicero* (Melbourne, 1954).

[2] R. M. Ogilvie's little book, *The Romans and their Gods* (London, 1969), is an admirable introduction, with further bibliography.

[3] 'The Religious Position of Livy's History', *JRS* lvii (1967), 45 ff.

[4] For Livy as a rationalizing sceptic in the mould of the Academic Cotta of Cicero's *ND* see J. Bayet, Budé Livy I, xxxix; as a Stoic rationalizer like Balbus, Walsh, 'Livy and Stoicism', *AJP* lxxix (1958), 355 ff.

[5] See in general I. Kajanto, *God and Fate in Livy* (Turku, 1957).

ties outside, for this is foreign to fundamental Roman notions of Roman deity. That deity lies essentially within the world, and achieves its ends by working through men.[1]

It is by visualizing this kind of cosmic harmony, in which human conduct is portrayed as affecting the course of the world, that we come closest to explaining Livy's state of mind when he presents prodigy-lists. We should not underestimate the literary effect of these entries in portraying an atmosphere of gloom; nor must one underplay the historian's criticism of the human credulity inspiring some of them. Yet when a sophisticated thinker like Livy punctiliously records these yearly lists in the face of current practice,[2] it is rash to assume that literary motives and occasional sceptical utterances explain all. He accepts the possibility that such prodigies express intimations of cosmic disorder or (in theological language) divine displeasure. They are occasioned by the earlier misbehaviour or aberrations of the body politic or of individuals within it, and accordingly are to be expiated with appropriate piety.[3]

c. *Livy and the Sources*

Livy's massive theme of the rise and moral decline of the Roman state precluded extensive primary research into the rich archival material available.[4] Then too his detached and philosophic attitude towards his subject is not characterized by that passion to unearth the precise details of 'what really happened' which marks the writing of a Polybius or a Tacitus. To gauge his neglect of the primary evidence, we need only examine his uncritical discussion of the evidence for Cornelius Cossus' *spolia opima*, or his cavalier attitude to the *libri lintei* in the first decade; or in the third his equally unhistorical attitude to the figures of Carthaginian troops obtained from the Lacinium column; or again, his failure to use the *senatus consultum de Bacchanalibus* in the fourth.[5]

---

[1] See vi. 18. 9, v. 11. 16.   [2] See xliii. 13. 1.

[3] On the prodigies in Livy see J. J. Delgado, 'Postura de Livio frente al prodigio', *Helmantica* xiv (1963), 383 ff., and 'Clasificación de los prodigios titolivianos', *Helmantica* xii (1961), 441 ff.; R. Bloch, *Les prodiges dans l'antiquité classique* (Paris, 1963); F. B. Krauss, *An Interpretation of the Omens, Portents and Prodigies recorded by Livy, Tacitus and Suetonius* (diss. Philadelphia, 1930). On the artistic presentation of prodigies in Livy see E. de Saint-Denis, 'Les énumerations des prodiges dans l'œuvre de Tite-Live', *RP* xvi (1942), 126 ff. On the history of Prodigy-literature see P. L. Schmidt's study (below, p. 22 n. 4).

[4] For the documentary evidence available see H. H. Scullard, *Roman Politics 220–150 B.C.* (Oxford, 1951), 251 ff.

[5] On Cossus' *spolia opima* see iv. 20. 5, with the useful discussions of Syme (p. 6 n. 1), Mensching (p. 6 n. 3), and Ogilvie (p. 6 n. 3). For the *libri lintei* see iv. 23. 2 and Ogilvie, 'Livy, Licinius Macer and the *Libri Lintei*', *JRS* xlviii (1958), 40 ff., a more sceptical view of the value of the *libri lintei* than mine. For the Lacinium column see Polybius iii. 33. 18 and 56. 4; Livy xxi. 38. 2 f. For the *s.c. de Bacchanalibus* see Livy xxxix. 8 ff. and *CIL* i. 196; D. W. L. van Son, *Livius' Behandeling von Bacchanalia* (Amsterdam, 1960, with English summary).

He is content to base his history on the evidence of secondary sources, with the result that all too often the value of his account fluctuates according to the reliability of the source followed in any particular section.

The most comprehensive research on Livy's sources has been published by A. Klotz.[1] By exploiting Livy's citation of his authorities,[2] and by study of the narrative of other historians recounting the same events, Klotz attempts to chart the historical sources for all the extant books. He rightly takes over the thesis of Nissen, whose 'law' postulates that Livy selects a single source for each section of his narrative; on this basis the historian builds up his own account, and appends any varying versions of fact provided by other sources which he consults.[3] Unfortunately, after meticulously assembling the available evidence Klotz too often dogmatically identifies a main source where a cautious *non liquet* would be more appropriate. His conclusions should therefore not be accepted uncritically.

The first decade is the most difficult. It is clear that here Livy used first-century authorities writing in Latin: Valerius Antias, Licinius Macer, Aelius Tubero, and (from the sixth book onwards) Claudius Quadrigarius.[4] He may also have consulted on occasion an earlier Latin annalist of the Gracchan era, L. Calpurnius Piso, who is cited five times in the decade, and Q. Fabius Pictor, the father of Roman history, whose work (composed in Greek) is quoted both under his name and under the label of *veterrimi auctores:* more probably, however, Livy made the acquaintance of these two at second hand in the work of Valerius Antias and Licinius Macer. The employment of these authorities has been well surveyed by Ogilvie for I–V (VI–X is a neglected area of Livian studies in this as in other respects), and Badian has provided useful thumbnail sketches;[5] more fundamental here is the outstanding research of H. Peter.[6]

The choice of sources for the third decade is clearer. For the cam-

---

[1] See *RE* xiii. 841 ff., and above all *Livius und seine Vorgänger* (Leipzig/Berlin, 1940–1), with full bibliography of Klotz's more specialized studies.

[2] These citations are collected by R. B. Steele, 'The Historical Attitude of Livy', *AJP* xxv (1904), 15 ff.

[3] H. Nissen, *Kritische Untersuchungen über die Quellen der vierten und fünften Dekade des Livius* (Berlin, 1868). The thesis is criticized by M. L. W. Laistner, *The Greater Roman Historians* (Berkeley, 1947), 83, but the evidence for it is overwhelming.

[4] See Th. Mommsen, *Hermes* v (1871), 270; W. Soltau, *Livius' Geschichtswerk, seine Composition und seine Quellen* (Leipzig, 1897). There is no substance in the suggestion of poetic sources for the early books, as claimed by M. Ghio, *RFIC* xxix (1951), 1 ff.; cf. H. Bardon, *REA* xliv (1942), 52 ff.

[5] Ogilvie, *Commentary*, 5 ff.; Badian (p. 11 n. 1), 18 ff. For greater detail on Claudius see M. Zimmerer, *Der Annalist Q. Claudius Quadrigarius* (diss. Munich, 1937); on Valerius Antias see Volkmann's article in *RE*.

[6] H. Peter, *Historicorum Romanorum Reliquiae*, I (Leipzig, 1870).

paigning in Italy and Spain the industrious monograph of Coelius Antipater is the basis, and for events in Greece, Sicily, and Africa there is evidence of the use of Polybius. The information gleaned from these two historians on the course of the war was supplemented from the researches of the first-century annalists Valerius Antias and Claudius Quadrigarius, who provided more systematic detail of deliberations, decisions, and appointments at Rome, as well as more circumstantial detail (usually unreliable) of events in the field. The two main and complementary sources are Coelius Antipater and Valerius Antias; Livy supplements the first from Polybius and the second from Claudius. In many places it is impossible to decide whether Livy is following Coelius or Polybius, for these writers utilized the same authorities, and to complicate matters further Coelius may have used Polybius as well. The safe procedure is to label the two contrasting bases of Livy's account 'Coelian/Polybian' and 'Valerian/Claudian'. The source-discussions of De Sanctis in his *Storia dei Romani* are particularly valuable for this decade.[1] For information on the sections stemming from Coelius/ Polybius, F. W. Walbank's bibliographical *Commentary on Polybius* is indispensable, and we now have the same scholar's Sather Lectures as well as Pédech's and Petzold's studies to inform us of the character of Polybius' work.[2] On Coelius Antipater there is Badian's useful contribution, and the short study of E. Wölfflin.[3]

For the fourth and fifth decades our knowledge of the sources is still more extensive, and Nissen and Kahrstedt long ago established the facts with close precision.[4] The fifteen extant books, covering the period 200–167 B.C., are concerned chiefly with the campaigns against Macedon, Aetolia, and Antiochus. In these eastern sections, which account for two-thirds of XXXI–XLV, Livy is content to rely on Polybius alone. (He had already taken stock of Polybius' accuracy and intelligence when composing the third decade, where he praises him laconically as 'haudquaquam spernendus auctor'.)[5] Hence Livy's version of these events in Greece and Asia can be labelled 'Polybius Romanized'.

These Polybian sections Livy integrates with the annalistic presentation of Valerius Antias and Claudius Quadrigarius, who provided him

[1] G. De Sanctis, *Storia dei Romani*, III 2 (Turin, 1917). See also F. Hellmann, *Livius-Interpretationen* (Berlin, 1939); W. Wiehemeyer, *Proben historiker Kritik aus Livius XXI–XLV* (diss. Münster, 1938).

[2] F. W. Walbank, *A Historical Commentary on Polybius*, I–II (Oxford, 1957–67), and *Polybius* (Berkeley, 1973): P. Pédech, *La méthode historique de Polybe* (Paris, 1964); K. E. Petzold, *Studien zur Methode des Polybios und zu ihrer historischen Ausvertlung* (Munich, 1969).

[3] Badian (p. 11 n. 1), 15 ff.; E. Wölfflin, *Antiochus von Syrakus und Coelius Antipater* (Winterthur, 1872), 22 ff.

[4] H. Nissen, see p. 14 n. 3; U. Kahrstedt, *Die Annalistik von Livius* (Berlin, 1913).

[5] xxx. 45. 5.

with fuller detail of Roman political events and of diplomatic and military detail in Northern Italy, Spain, and Africa. As in the earlier decades, Klotz here overschematizes when he suggests that Livy prefers to follow Valerius Antias up to the trials of the Scipios in XXXVIII, and that subsequently he prefers Claudius Quadrigarius.[1] The evidence of the earlier decades suggests that Livy continually consulted both, but Valerius Antias more prominently. One other author was probably consulted in the fourth decade, M. Porcius Cato, whose *Origines* was available for detail of Cato's Spanish campaigning. The evidence—a scathing reference by Livy to Cato's immodest boasting, and linguistic similarities—is not conclusive, for Livy's encounter with Cato's work could have been at second hand through the work of Valerius Antias or Claudius Quadrigarius, but the unusual extent and detail here certainly reflect Cato's personal testimony.[2]

What sources did Livy follow in the lost sections of his work? Obviously he continued to use Polybius within the framework of the late annalists for the remainder of his fifth decade. Poseidonius' *Histories* began where Polybius ended, and covered the period from 146 to the dictatorship of Sulla in 88; Sempronius Asellio's history in Latin also covered the years 146–91, so that in the sixth and seventh decades Livy could have used Asellio and Poseidonius together with the late annalists,[3] much as he had exploited Polybius and Coelius Antipater in the third decade; and the phraseology of the *Periochae* suggests that Sallust's *Bellum Jugurthinum* was additionally used for the African events of 118–104 B.C. For the eighth and ninth decades (91–78 B.C.), there was Sisenna's admired work, which Livy could have complemented with Sulla's *Commentarii*.[4] Thereafter Livy could have based his work on Sallust's *Historiae* (which documented the years 78–66 B.C.), and the same historian's *Bellum Catilinae*; Caesar's *Commentarii* and their continuation by Hirtius; Asinius Pollio's seventeen books, which covered the period 60–42 B.C.; and Augustus' own memoirs. But our information about available histories for the period after 42 is meagre.[5]

---

[1] A. Klotz, 'Zu den Quellen der vierten und fünften Dekade des Livius', *Hermes* l (1915), 481 ff.

[2] xxxiv. 8 f., 11 ff. Livy calls Cato 'haud sane detractator laudum suarum'. Most scholars support H. Peter's thesis (*HRR* CI ff.) that Livy consults Cato directly, most recently H. Tränkle, 'Catos *Origines* im Geschichtswerk des Livius', *Festschr. K. Büchner* (Wiesbaden, 1970), 274 ff. I. Paschowski, *Die Kunst der Reden in der 4. und 5. Dekade des Livius* (diss. Kiel, 1966), 107 ff., examines the speech at xxxiv. 2 ff. to show stylistic parallels with Cato's fragments.

[3] Poseidonius does not seem to have been used for the Gracchan period (E. Meyer, *Kleine Schriften*, I [Halle, 1910], 421). The citations of Valerius Antias and Claudius Quadrigarius by Orosius (v. 16, v. 20) suggest that Livy was still following these annalists for the late second and early first century.

[4] So E. Badian, *JRS* l (1962), 48 ff.

[5] For Livy's use of Pollio compare the two accounts of Cicero's death, which have

D. *The First Decade*

After this brief survey of Livy's over-all interpretation, his religious and moral preconceptions, and the sources on which he based his account, we can review the extant decades successively as historical documents.

At the outset of his work Livy had to make a difficult choice. Should he include the legendary history of Rome's early years, or should he emulate Claudius Quadrigarius, and begin more soberly after the Gallic sack of 387/6? For a variety of reasons—chiefly, we may presume, patriotic pride and the Augustan pleasure in antiquarianism—he chose to begin with the shadowy beginning, duly warning his readers not to regard the first sections as sober history.[1] Scholars have reacted to his decision according to their cast of mind and the spirit of their age. The condemnation of an earlier generation of historians like Mommsen and Pais has been followed by the more positive approach of contemporary scholars; emphasis is now being laid on the solid core of historical reality underlying the legendary anecdotes.

The spectacular discoveries of archaeologists have done much to win this new respect for the essential historicity of the tradition. R. Bloch has written a useful survey of the political, social, and religious evidence which archaeology offers on Rome as a Latin settlement, on the period of Etruscan dominance, and on the conditions after the Etruscan departure; he fruitfully compares this with the traditional literary version set out in Livy's first two books.[2] This book also explains the main lines of controversy about the foundation of Rome between Gjerstad and Pallottino, also surveyed in a magisterial article by A. Momigliano.[3] Vigorous controversy continues over the wide range of problems connected with the Regal period and the early Republic.[4]

The historical problems arising from the third to the tenth books have naturally enough not received such concentrated attention. Ogilvie's *Commentary* (with the *Addenda* of the second impression) covers the first five books, and the Budé volumes containing the excellent historical appendices of J. Bayet and R. Bloch have reached VII. Erich Burck has published a paper which usefully sketches Livy's portrayal of Rome

survived in Seneca's *Suasoriae*. On the paucity of documentation for history on the period 42 B.C. onwards see Syme (p. 5 n. 1), 64 ff.

[1] *Praef.* 6.

[2] R. Bloch, *Tite-Live et les premiers siècles de Rome* (Paris, 1965); cf. his earlier book, *The Origins of Rome* (London, 1960), and his article in *REL* xxxvii (1959), 118 ff.

[3] 'An Interim Report on the Origins of Rome', *JRS* liii (1963), 95 ff.

[4] Add to Ogilvie's bibliographies A. Werner, *Der Beginn der römischen Republik* (Munich, 1963); H. Tränkle, 'Der Anfang des römisches Freistaaats in der Darstellung des Livius', *Hermes* xciii (1965), 311 ff.; R. E. A. Palmer, *The Archaic Community of the Romans* (Cambridge, 1970); A. Alföldi, *Early Rome and the Latins* (Ann Arbor, 1965); J. Heurgon, *The Rise of Rome* (London, 1972); and the papers in *Les origines de la république romaine* (Fondation Hardt vol. xiii, 1967).

in VI–X.[1] The historical basis of the account of Rome's struggles with the Samnites is discussed in Salmon's monograph and in an article by A. Klotz.[2] There are numerous articles on restricted topics within the decade, several from the pen of E. Burck.[3]

The central question of the historical value of the account of the years from the foundation to 293 B.C. has been briefly tackled by J. Briscoe.[4] The outline of the military operations undertaken by the growing Republic may be regarded as acceptable, though the detail of individual engagements is usually fictitious; but the historian himself seems insufficiently aware of the strategy of systematic expansion throughout the peninsula.[5] A similar judgement can be passed on the version of Roman domestic history. Though his narrative of the human circumstances within which the social and constitutional changes are described contains little reliable fact, the general outline of the changes is accepted by modern historians with a few qualifications. In particular, Livy does not distinguish sufficiently between the political and the economic aspects of the plebeian agitation, and the various stages of the legislation marking concessions to the plebeians are confused.[6]

E. *The Third Decade*

This section of the *Ab Urbe Condita* is the best by which to study Livy's historical achievement. On the one hand there are reasonably adequate sources from which to elicit what really happened; unlike the first decade, the third contains little fabulous content. On the other hand greater efforts of interpretation and synthesis are required than in the fourth and fifth decades, where Livy is chiefly adapting the information from a single source. Moreover, the theme of the Second Punic War engaged his historical imagination and patriotic pride more than any other. The decade as a whole has been well analysed by E. Burck.[7]

---

[1] E. Burck, 'Zum Rombild des Livius-Interpretationen zur zweiten Pentade', in *Vom Menschenbild in der römischen Literatur* (Heidelberg, 1966), 321 ff.

[2] E. T. Salmon, *Samnium and the Samnites* (Cambridge, 1967); A. Klotz, 'Livius' Darstellung des zweiter Samniterkrieges', *Mnem.* 3rd series vi (1938), 87 ff.

[3] See especially the papers by Pareti, Funaioli, Niccolini, and others in *Studi Liviani* (Rome, 1934). On the early books see Burck, 'Die Frühgeschichte Roms bei Livius im Lichte der Denkmaler', *Gymn.* lxxv (1968), 74 ff. On Camillus see Burck in *Wege zu Livius*, 310 ff.; Momigliano in *CQ* xxxvi (1942), 111 ff. On Manlius Capitolinus (Livy vi. 11–20) see Burck, *Gymn.* lxxiii (1966), 94 ff.; on the Second Samnite War see K-H. Schwarte, *Historia* xx (1971), 368 ff. Earlier studies are listed in K. Gries (p. 3 n. 1), 69 ff.

[4] In *Livy* (p. 3 n. 5), ch. 1.

[5] See Bayet's Appendix I to the Budé edition of VII.

[6] See Briscoe (p. 18 n. 4), 8 ff.; Scullard, *A History of the Roman World 753–146 B.C.* (London, 1951), 92 ff. and Appendix 6.

[7] Most recently in *Livy* (p. 3 n. 5), ch. 2, and at greater length in *Einführung in die dritte Dekade des Livius* (Heidelberg, 1950). W. Hoffmann's *Livius und der zweite punische Krieg* (Berlin, 1942), deserves greater attention than it has received. See also

Livy's treatment is inevitably one-sided. The absence of information about the Carthaginian administration—its discussions are recorded only five times before XXX, and in a tendentious manner—is the more blatant because of the abundance of information on senatorial and executive activities at Rome. Then too his accounts of the various campaigns reveal his shortcomings as a military historian; the narratives of Italian, Spanish, Greek, Sicilian, and African operations reflect his characteristic weaknesses in topography, tactics, and numerical esti-mates of numbers involved. On the credit side is the conscientious yearly documentation of the commanders and the forces allotted to them in each area of campaigning; there can be few war-histories in the whole of European history with such voluminous information about the strategic planning from the centre.[1] There is likewise an extraordi-nary range of social and economic information, though no attempt is made to synthesize or interpret this evidence collectively.[2] Diplomatic exchanges between Rome and other states are also systematically recorded, with formal agreements and treaties set down apparently verbatim; unfortunately Livy has too often incorporated chauvinistic distortion from the late annalistic sources, as in his version of the treaty of the Ebro and of the peace concluded at the end of the war.[3]

Clearly the faults enunciated here are attributable to over-reliance on the biased late sources, and to the lack of a sufficiently critical judgement which prefers, for example, a version dating the fall of Saguntum to 218 rather than to Polybius' date of 219, so that the whole chronology of the Spanish events in XXI becomes confused, and the events distorted.[4] Livy's failure to detach himself sufficiently from the source-material brings the further limitation that he fails to stamp each section of his history with a clear personal interpretation. He never attempts, for example, any systematic explanation of the factors which helped Rome to victory in the Second Punic War. As has been suggested earlier, his obsession is with moral causation. For Livy the implicit causes of the

my forthcoming 'Livy and the Aims of *historia*; An Analysis of the third Decade', in *Aufstieg und Niedergang der römischen Welt* (ed. H. Temporini), vol. II.

[1] The reliability of this evidence is defended most recently by A. J. Toynbee, *Hannibal's Legacy* (London, 1965), II. 36 ff.; E. Rawson, 'Prodigy Lists and the use of the *Annales Maximi*', *CQ* N.S. xxi (1971), 138 ff., illustrates from inconsistencies and curiosities in the prodigy-lists the inherent improbability that this material comes from the *annales maximi*, and so reinforces the scepticism of M. Gelzer, *Hermes* lxx (1935), 269 ff. = *Kl. Schr.* III (Wiesbaden, 1964), 220 ff., about the accuracy of the military information. One has always to admit the possibility of fictitious additions, but the divergences from Polybius are not numerous.

[2] See my essay in *Latin Historians* (p. 3 n. 5), 128 = *Wege zu Livius*, 249 ff.

[3] For such issues as these the most useful systematic work of reference is Walbank's *Commentary on Polybius* (p. 15 n. 2).

[4] See the useful articles of G. V. Sumner in *PACA* ix (1966), 5 ff., and *HSCP* lxxii (1968), 205 ff., and my edition of XXI (Cambridge, 1973).

Roman victory are the qualities of its great leaders, especially Scipio Africanus, Fabius Maximus Cunctator, Claudius Marcellus; he is less concerned with the political and economic factors which gave Rome an increasingly solid base for the prosecution of the war. In this sense the characterization of these and of other important Roman figures on the one side, and of Hannibal on the other, is of central importance.[1]

F. *The Fourth and Fifth Decades*[2]

For the years 200–167 B.C. Livy is pre-eminently concerned with Macedonia, Greece, and Asia. Though he systematically records the recurring revolts against Roman dominance in Cisalpine Gaul, Sardinia and Corsica, and Spain, together with the diplomatic crises in Africa arising from the tensions between Masinissa and the Carthaginians, these topics rarely get extended attention. In the year-by-year survey of Roman interests in the Mediterranean, the historian's main concern is with eastern operations.

For these eastern events Livy was content to rely on the authority of Polybius alone, and since long sections of Polybius' *Histories* have survived, it is possible to look over Livy's shoulder and see him at work presenting the facts for a Roman audience. The systematic comparison between Greek and Roman versions provides the clearest insight into Livy's mind, and answers a range of important questions. How honest is Livy? How good is his Greek? What facts does he omit, and what extra information does he provide, for a Roman audience? What are the literary principles on which he structures his account?[3]

In general Livy emerges from such an inquiry into his honesty with some credit, if we consider the abysmal standards of truthfulness which he inherited from the late annalists. But his thesis that 'nulla umquam respublica nec maior nec sanctior nec bonis exemplis ditior

---

[1] See Burck in *Livy* (p. 3 n. 5), 31 ff. On Scipio Africanus in Livy see H. H. Scullard, *Scipio Africanus Soldier and Politician* (London, 1970), 25 ff.; on Hannibal see J. Vogt, *Das Hannibal-Portrait im Geschichtswerk des T. Livius unde seine Ursprünge* (diss. Freiburg, 1953). For articles on specialized topics in this decade see Gries (p. 3 n. 1), 69 ff.

[2] The excellent chapter of Walbank, 'The Fourth and Fifth Decades', in *Livy* (p. 3 n. 5) should above all be consulted. J. Briscoe's *Commentary on XXXI–XXXIII* (Oxford, 1973) will help to stimulate interest in this neglected area. Two dissertations by pupils of E. Burck are devoted to Livy's presentation and thought in these decades: H. Brüggmann, *Komposition und Entwicklungstendenzen der Bücher 31–35 des Titus Livius* (Kiel, 1954), and F. Kern, *Aufbau und Gedankengang der Bücher 36–45* (Kiel, 1960). P. Jal's Budé edition of XLI–XLII (p. 8 n. 6) contains an excellent Introduction and more copious annotation than has been customary in the series. The recent Italian edition of XLI–XLV and the fragments by G. Pascucci (Turin, 1970) has a substantial Introduction. For specialized articles see Gries (p. 3 n. 1), 73 ff.

[3] Having begun my own Livy researches with such a Polybius–Livy comparison at the prompting of Professor F. W. Walbank, I am convinced of its value as a means of disciplined investigation of Livy's aims and techniques.

fuit'[1] leads him to idealize the conduct of the Roman senate and armies, and likewise the behaviour of Roman leaders; and this betrays him into occasional suppressions and distortions of awkward facts. Clear examples of this are provided by Walbank and by E. Pianezzola.[2] But whilst acknowledging Livy's culpability in these respects we should not inflate occasional peccadilloes into systematic dishonesty, for Livy's handling of the Polybian evidence is substantially fair and accurate. A similar judgement may be made of his abilities as translator. He undoubtedly makes mistakes, some crass and some ridiculous, but there are not many when they are measured against the vast amount of material which he had to translate.[3]

Of great interest are the many passages which Livy expands or abbreviates in the interests of a different audience from Polybius'. He explains religious and political customs and titles, points of geography and history, military terminology, and so on—and occasionally comes to grief in doing so.[4] The questions of his literary techniques as they emerge from comparison with Polybius we may postpone for more general scrutiny.

In these 'Polybian' sections, Livy is usually as good as his source—and therefore essentially reliable. In his description of Italian, Spanish, and African events, where his authorities are the late annalists, the same slavish tendencies necessitate an opposite estimate. Nissen's classic paradox—the more circumstantial the account, the more suspect it must be—can be vindicated merely by analysis of Livy's recurring formulations. Occasional Roman defeats are followed by inevitable victories. Cliché-ridden situations are described in cliché-ridden language. The geography and topography are invariably vague, the size of enemy casualties massive and crudely repetitive. The detail of diplomatic exchanges and agreements is likewise unreliable, for the factual substratum is adorned with chauvinistic additions.[5] Modern historians accordingly tend to sup at these banquests with long spoons, judging each issue on the inherent probabilities rather than on the detailed claims reproduced by Livy from these biased sources.[6]

---

[1] *Praef.* 11.

[2] Walbank (p. 20 n. 2), 54 f.; E. Pianezzola, *Traduzione e Ideologia; Livio Interprete di Polibio* (Bologna, 1969), ch. 3. Cf. Walsh, *AJP* lxxvi (1955), 369 ff.

[3] See Walsh, *GR* N.S. v (1958), 83 ff.; Walbank (p. 20 n. 2), 54 f.; for a spirited defence of Livy see J. A. de Foucault, 'Tite-Live traducteur de Polybe', *REL* xlvi (1968), 208 ff.

[4] Pianezzola (p. 21 n. 2), ch. 2; the blind leading the blind, Walbank (p. 20 n. 2), 56.

[5] On these annalistic sections see H. Nissen (p. 14 n. 3) and U. Kahrstedt (p. 15 n. 4). As one glaring example, the problems of Carthaginian–Numidian relations in Africa, see Walsh, 'Masinissa', *JRS* lv (1965), 149 ff. K. E. Petzold, *Die Eröffnung des zweiten römisch-makedonischen Krieges; Untersuchung zur spätannalistischen Topik bei Livius* (Berlin, 1940), considers the annalistic section at the start of the fourth decade.

[6] See, for example, E. Badian, *Foreign Clientelae* (Oxford, 1958); M. Gelzer, *Kleine Schriften*, III 272.

G. *The Summaries and the Livian Tradition*

Over three-quarters of Livy's work (XI–XX, XLVI–CXLII) has been lost, chiefly because few individuals sought to acquire and read the whole history; an 'essential Livy' existed as early as A.D. 100.[1] The surviving *Periochae*, conventionally dated to the fourth century and covering the entire work except CXXXVI–VII, have been indifferently edited by O. Rossbach, and the Oxyrhynchus epitome (embracing summaries of XXXVII–XL and XLVIII–LV) has a commentary by E. Kornemann.[2] The nature of the *Periochae* and their provenance have been examined by C. M. Begbie, who astringently demolishes assumed theories and demonstrates our ignorance of this twilight world.[3] P. L. Schmidt has extended the scope of the discussion to consider the connection between Livy's text, the two epitomes, and the writers of the Livian tradition, with a full account of earlier theories.[4]

The relationship of Livy with these writers of the Livian tradition (Florus, Granius Licinianus, Aurelius Victor, Eutropius, Festus, Orosius, Cassiodorus, Julius Obsequens) still awaits comprehensive treatment, but individual studies have clarified the situation. In addition to Schmidt's book just mentioned, we have Eadie's critical edition of Festus, and Jal's excellent Introduction to his Budé text of Florus.[5] Millar's scepticism about the possibility of establishing definitive connections between Cassius Dio and his sources (in the face of the common belief that Livy is a main source) should also be noted.[6]

---

[1] Mart. xiv. 190.

[2] Rossbach's text, which appears in the Teubner Livy Volume 4 (1910) and is reproduced in Vol. XIV of the Loeb edition, is acutely criticized in the Ph.D. dissertation of R. A. Reid, 'The Manuscript Tradition of the Periochae of Livy' (Cambridge, 1969, unpublished). For the Oxyrhynchus epitome see E. Kornemann, *Die neue Livius-Epitome aus Oxyrhynchus* (Leipzig, 1904).

[3] C. M. Begbie, 'The Epitome of Livy', *CQ* N.s. xvii (1967), 332 ff.

[4] P. L. Schmidt, *Iulius Obsequens und das Problem der Livius-Epitome* (Mainz, 1968).

[5] J. W. Eadie, *The Breviarium of Festus* (London, 1967), 70 ff.; P. Jal in his edition of Florus (Paris, 1967). Another useful contribution is W. K. Sherwin's 'Livy and the *De viris illustribus*', *Philol.* cxiii (1969), 298 ff.

[6] Fergus Millar, *A Study of Cassius Dio* (Oxford, 1964), 34 ff., in reaction against such assumptions as those of E. Schwartz in *RE*.

III. LIVY AS LITERARY ARTIST

CRITICS nowadays are reluctant to separate historian and writer in any schematic way, but such an approach is justified in the case of Roman rhetorical historiography One fundamental cause of the lack of rigour amongst many Roman historians in ascertaining the truth is the first-century notion that 'history' is a description of the manner of writing rather than of scrupulousness of research. L. Ferrero reminds us[1] that when Cicero describes history as 'opus . . . unum hoc oratorium maxime' he is claiming for the orator a general competence in eloquence, written no less than spoken, which is his professional qualification: 'physica ista ipsa et mathematica et quae paulo ante ceterarum artium propria posuisti, scientiae sunt eorum qui illa profitentur; illustrari autem oratione si quis istas ipsas artes velit, ad oratoris ei confugiendum est facultatem.'[2] The orator has been trained to give public expression to all kinds of knowledge, including historical analysis. Livy may not have practised at the bar, but he is an orator in this theoretical sense, trained in the science of words.

A. *The Annalistic Framework*

In a paper of fundamental importance for the literary aspects of Livian studies, McDonald rightly insists that study of the historian's presentation must begin with the annalistic framework.[3] Livy structures his history in the yearly blocks which ensure the requisite chronological clarity. Each year begins with the inauguration of the magistrates and the allocation of the provinces; then, after a systematic survey of the year's events at home and abroad, he returns to Rome to complete the annals of the year with further information, political and sacral—in particular, elections and prodigy-lists. The Latin of this annalistic framework is deliberately jejune and formulaic, as if to emphasize the authenticity of these catalogues by the evocation of the old registers, the *annales maximi*.[4] To these lists is frequently appended the detail of antique religious ceremonial, in which Livy's diction is tinged with formal archaism, and of the political debates which exercised a compelling fascination on the patriotic antiquarianism of the Augustan age.[5]

---

[1] In his useful collection of papers on Roman historiography, *Rerum scriptor; saggi sulla storiografia romana* (Trieste, 1962), 21 ff.　　　[2] *De Leg.* i. 2. 5, 14. 61.

[3] A. H. McDonald, 'The Style of Livy', *JRS* xlvii (1957), 155 ff.

[4] On which see J. E. A. Crake, 'The Annals of the Pontifex Maximus', *CP* xxxv (1940), 375 ff.; and E. Rawson (p. 19 n. 1).

[5] Important for this aspect is the work of W. Kroll, *Studien zum Verständnis der römischen Literatur* (Stuttgart, 1924), 331 ff.

B. *The Internal Structure*

Within the annalistic framework Livy follows the Ciceronian principles of *exaedificatio* and *exornatio*—again McDonald's paper is our guide— to build up and to adorn his narrative. Fundamental to the understanding of his craftsmanship is an awareness that he composes each section on the basis of a single source. Clearly the degree of labour and rigour involved depended on the nature of the particular source followed. His central concerns, especially in military contexts, were clarification of time and place; description of planning, action, and outcome; and explanation of human qualities or defects which had produced this result.[1] It is probable that most of the historical works utilized for the extant books required no extensive restructuring in these directions. We observe that when following Polybius Livy saw no need to recast the material in any major way, since the Greek historian so admirably embodies the Ciceronian ideal; accordingly he can concentrate on the insertion of brief clarifications, on excisions of material he considers superfluous for his readers, and on touches of dramatic elaboration.[2] He had more to do when he used the late annalists, especially when he had to reconcile their chronology with Polybius', but it is impossible to establish how much of the psychological analysis which is Livy's central interest was already present in these Latin sources.

In his *exaedificatio* Livy sought as far as possible to divide the material into self-contained sections. Burck well sets out the principles by which the historian constructs these scenes with an Aristotelian beginning, middle, and end, and he provides instructive examples of such *Einzelerzählungen* by comparison with Dionysius of Halicarnassus, thus clarifying and extending the researches earlier achieved by K. Witte's comparison with Polybius in the third and fourth decades.[3] These episodes—sieges, battles, political debates, personal adventures, and so on— can usually be described in one rounded section. But others are of a more extended nature, and these Livy often attempts to present as a developing drama in self-contained acts; the sieges of Saguntum and Abydus are cases in point, as also in the first decade is the annihilation of the Fabii at Cremera.[4] This technique of frequent division of the narrative

---

[1] See Cic. *De Or.* ii. 63, and above, p. 11 n. 2.

[2] One may observe such elaboration at many points in the fourth decade where Polybius is the source; see my *Livy*, 186 ff. Or again, study his version of Hannibal's dream at xxi. 22 against the source Coelius Antipater, which happens to have survived (in Cic. *Div.* i. 49).

[3] E. Burck, *Die Erzählungskunst* (p. 8 n. 2); K. Witte, 'Über die Form der Darstellung in Livius' Geschichtswerk', *RhM* lxv (1910), 270 ff., 359 ff.

[4] xxi. 7–15; xxxi. 17–18; ii. 23–33.

into episodes does not result in total fragmentation, for Livy is adept at linking these scenes by artistic techniques of connection.[1]

Livy's history after the early books is 'pragmatic' history, concerned overwhelmingly with war and politics. For this reason certain types of event repeatedly recur, and Livy develops standardized patterns of presentation for them. I have elsewhere tried to outline recurrent techniques of siege- and battle-descriptions; and within these schematized sections Livy shows how he has profited from Caesar's techniques of dramatic narrative. As in military contexts, so also in political and diplomatic narratives; he has favourite methods of describing the psychological reactions of assemblies, or again the confrontations between Roman and foreign leaders.[2]

In such military and political scenes Livy's main aim is to depict the psychology of the participants: besieged communities facing slavery or death, armies and their generals under pressure of impending defeat, assemblies reacting to national failure or success, state-leaders probing in discussion each other's moral resources. These situations are dramatized by concentration on the feelings and reactions of the participants, and for this reason the label of 'tragic' history has often been attached to his work. The controversy surrounding 'tragic' history as it affects Hellenistic historians like Duris and Phylarchus is well known. Schwartz and Scheller argued that these writers developed their 'tragic' approach under the influence of Peripatetic theory; B. L. Ullman preferred to categorize it as part of the legacy of Isocrates. Walbank has competently reviewed the arguments in a thoughtful rebuttal of the latest apologist for the 'Peripatetic' theory, K. von Fritz.[3] Erich Burck earlier attempted to establish Livy as heir to such 'Peripatetic' aims and techniques; he has now reviewed the controversy,[4] with the limited aim of stressing structural similarities between the Hellenistic histories dominated by Aristotelian dramatic theory and Livy's principles of composition. This is reasonable enough, as indeed is the claim that there is a close connection between the historian's techniques of dramatic narrative and the effects sought by the Greek tragedians. It is the label 'Peripatetic' which is gratuitous, for there is evidence of this kind of dramatic historical writing before Aristotle, and it is subsumed within a tradition of Hellenistic rhetorical historiography too broad for this restrictive definition.

[1] Walsh, *Livy*, 180 f.; Walbank (p. 20 n. 2), 59 f.

[2] On the military contexts see H. Bruckmann, *Die römischen Niederlagen im Geschichtswerk des T. Livius* (diss. Münster, 1936). In general see Walsh, *Livy*, ch. 8, and *RhM* xcvii (1954), 97 ff.

[3] F. W. Walbank, 'History and Tragedy', *Historia* ix (1960), 216 ff., with bibliography of earlier contributions to the controversy.

[4] Earlier in *Die Erzählungskunst* (p. 8 n. 2); more recently in 'Wahl und Anordnung des Stoffes: Führung der Handlung' in *Wege zu Livius* (p. 3 n. 6), 331 ff.

c. *Style and Presentation in Dramatic Narrative*

The structural principles on which Livy builds up his narrative-scenes dictate the basis of his style. Of particular value for the study of his narrative-presentation are the comprehensive book of J-P. Chausserie-Laprée and the published thesis of K. Lindemann.[1] These scholars demonstrate how the introductory sentence of a section, with its detail of 'acteur, lieu, notation temporelle', can be classified in particular patterns. Frequently there is a temporal connection with the previous scene ('dum haec geruntur', 'sub idem fere tempus', 'per eosdem forte dies', etc.). Again, the intentions of the character concerned are often indicated in what Lindemann calls the '*ratus*-Periode', with the 'psychological' participle characteristically preceding the main verb. So too Livy has regular ways of ending a section, often with a brief statement of the 'haec eo anno acta' type.

Within this frame Livy skilfully assembles the events of a scene with a combination of longer period-sentences and short statements. Often the longer period-sentences are deployed as an economical technique of explaining the preliminaries to the main action, which is then described with the dramatic texture of short sentences, historic infinitives or historic presents, and other devices. Of particular interest in warfare-narrative is the way in which Livy achieves artistic balance in describing the activities of opposing forces; McDonald rightly insists on the importance of this alternation of action, represented syntactically, as the key to much of Livy's narrative composition, and I have tried to illustrate this technique elsewhere.[2]

Chausserie-Laprée devotes close attention to the structure of the Livian 'period'; comparative study with other Roman historians demonstrates its similarities to Caesarean usage, while establishing the greater versatility of Livy as a stylist.[3] Thus the French scholar rightly emphasizes the subtle *variatio* with which Livy rings the changes on the basic scheme of the alternation of subordinate clauses and participial expressions leading to the climax of the main verb.

---

[1] J-P. Chausserie-Laprée, *L'expression narrative chez les historiens latins* (Paris, 1969); Klaus Lindemann, *Beobachtungen zur livianischen Periodenkunst* (Marburg, 1964).

[2] McDonald (p. 23 n. 3), 165; Walsh, *Livy*, 250 ff., and *Latin Historians* (p. 3 n. 5), 130 f. We should perhaps drop the description 'periodic' for this varied texture; see L. P. Wilkinson's protest in *Golden Latin Artistry* (Cambridge, 1963), 186.

[3] Lindemann (p. 26 n. 1), 148 ff. has a useful section on 'Livius und Caesar'. The wider ramifications of Caesar's influence have not been systematically studied, but cf. A. Klotz, 'Caesar und Livius', *RhM* xcvi (1953), 62 ff.

D. *Opus oratorium maxime*

Within the general significance of the Ciceronian dictum that historio-graphy is 'the task for orators' there is the more particular sense in which the historian must manifest the orator's skills. In spite of occa-sional protests from Greeks like Polybius or Romans like Pompeius Trogus,[1] ancient historians from Herodotus to Tacitus remained con-vinced of the broad historical value of composed speeches attributed to individual leaders at important junctures; Cicero recommends the prac-tice, which survives beyond the classical era.[2] In some ancient historians like Thucydides such speeches can be fruitfully analysed as meditative reflections on the human situation in particular circumstances of per-sonal crisis or political change, and some scholars suggest that Livy's speeches compare badly with those of Thucydides in this respect.[3] But Livy's primary aim in his speeches is not so much general philosophical reflection as historical characterization; the speech is the main vehicle for his didactic lesson, which in the extant books is to help the reader understand 'per quos viros quibusque artibus domi militiaeque et partum et auctum imperium sit'.[4]

To comprehend how Livy achieves this characterizing aim the reader must first study Roman rhetorical theory, and observe how all Livy's speeches with one or two exceptions are structured according to the 'rules' for the *genus deliberativum*. Our most informative guide here is R. Ullmann, who has studied Livy's speeches in two useful monographs.[5] It is particularly enlightening to place Livy's composed versions side by side with the speeches in his source Polybius, for by this means we are enabled to observe the extent of the restructuring; Livy introduces an *exordium* and a *conclusio* if the Greek version plunges *in medias res* or ends abruptly, and he delineates the attitudes of the speaker and em-phasizes the significance of the occasion by new or enhanced motifs in the *tractatio*.[6] I. Paschkowski has been able, by analysis of Cato's speech in XXXIV, to demonstrate how Livy not merely illuminates Cato's basic attitudes but also captures his idiom; and in examination of the speech of Aemilius Paullus in XLV (where comparison with Appian,

---

[1] Pol. xii. 25a. 5; Pompeius Trogus ap. Iustin. xxxviii. 3. 11: 'in Livio et in Sallustio reprehendit quod contiones directas pro sua ratione operi suo inserendo historiae modum excesserint.' On Trogus' relation to Livy see R. B. Steele, *AJP* xxxviii (1917), 19 ff.

[2] *Or.* 66. The great twelfth-century British historian William of Malmesbury is a good example of a medieval writer who composes speeches to adorn his history.

[3] I document such criticism in my *Livy*, 220 n. 2.

[4] *Praef.* 9.

[5] For the *genus deliberativum* see above all Quint. iii. 4. 15; and R. Ullmann, *La technique des discours dans Salluste, Tite-Live et Tacite* (Oslo, 1927); *Étude sur le style des discours de Tite-Live* (Oslo, 1929).

[6] See my *Livy*, 219 ff., building on the foundation of Ullmann's work.

Diodorus, and Plutarch is possible) she shows Livy emphasizing the more traditional Roman qualities.[1] In another Kiel dissertation R. Treptow has concentrated in a similar way on speeches in the first and third decades; and E. Burck, capitalizing on the work of Treptow and of W. Hoffmann, has given detailed attention to the speech of Scipio Africanus delivered to the mutineers in Spain, to the orations of Scipio and Hannibal before Zama, and to the speeches at the Aetolian Council in 200 B.C.[2] The speeches of Scipio Africanus and Hannibal before Zama, like the earlier pair of speeches delivered by Scipio *père* and Hannibal at the outset of the war in Italy, offer useful instruction on how the ancient historian can characterize leaders by *comparison* of their words; where Livy finds such juxtaposition already present in his source, he both seeks greater artistic balance in length and argumentation, and sharpens the elements of contrasting characterization.

Like Polybius, Livy records some speeches in *oratio recta*, some in *oratio obliqua*, and some in a combination of both, breaking into *oratio recta* to achieve greater rhetorical impact. The statistics explaining the length and frequency of the different patterns of speech are tabulated in the work of O. Kohl, and summarized by H. Bornecque.[3] Of chief interest here are the artistic principles on which Livy bases these different methods of reporting. A. Lambert has devoted a monograph[4] to Livy's use of indirect speech. The subject has an importance lying deeper than considerations of mere style; it is instructive to note how frequently the historian exploits such indirect discourse to probe the thought-processes of individuals and groups, when no words were actually spoken, so that this forms an important method of characterization. Where actual speeches are recorded, it is difficult to establish precise criteria by which *oratio recta* is preferred to *oratio obliqua* or vice versa. Older scholars have been mistaken in assuming that Livy uses *oratio obliqua* to express an argument non-rhetorically, or again that when the two are in juxtaposition the *oratio recta* represents Livy's own sentiments. Lambert's study is particularly useful for its analysis of Livy's subtle stylistic variation in reported speech, which he illustrates by judicious comparison with Polybius, Caesar, and Sallust.

In the direct speeches the rhetorical techniques of Livy are classified

---

[1] I. Paschkowski, *Die Kunst der Reden in der 4. und 5. Dekade des Livius* (diss. Kiel, 1966).

[2] R. Treptow, *Die Kunst der Reden in der 1. und 3. Dekade des livianischen Geschichtswerks* (Kiel, 1964); E. Burck, *Wege zu Livius* (p. 3 n. 6), 430 ff.; for Hoffmann's book see p. 18 n. 7.

[3] O. Kohl, 'Über Zweck und Bedeutung der livianischen Reden', *Jahresbericht über die Realschule und das Gymnasium zu Barmen* (Barmen, 1872); Bornecque (p. 7 n. 6), ch. 14.

[4] A. Lambert, *Die indirekte Rede als künstlerisches Stilmittel des Livius* (diss. Zürich, 1946).

in two papers by H. V. Canter, whose work was extended by the contributions of R. Ullmann.[1] In a further article Ullmann has examined also the clausulae in Livy's speeches.[2]

E. *Latinity*

In this section the topics of diction, syntax, and prose-rhythms in narrative are arbitrarily segregated from the earlier section on narrative-style. In general, it is important to distinguish between the Latinity of the speeches and that of the narrative. In the speeches, as has been noted, the texture is consciously Ciceronian; we are here concerned with the Latin of the narrative. This area of study is still dominated by the work of the great nineteenth-century philologues.

In the study of Livian diction the theory that has exercised greatest influence was that propounded first by E. Wölfflin and developed by his pupil, S. G. Stacey.[3] These scholars believed that Livy in the first decade was creating a new historical style, deploying a more poetic vocabulary and seeking a wider variety of expression, but that subsequently in the third and still more in the fourth and fifth decades he reverted to the more orthodox norms of golden Latinity. The thesis was widely accepted; it is incorporated, for example, in Palmer's standard work on the Latin language, and though scholars like Löfstedt and Burck have offered more subtle psychological explanations for such a reversion, the central argument was unchallenged.[4] The first shots across its bows were fired by K. Gries, who demonstrated that many 'poetic' usages cited by Stacey were not in fact poetic, and that others claimed for the first decade only do in fact recur in the later decades.[5]

More recently in a notable article H. Tränkle[6] has overturned the whole thesis. He assembles one set of 'archaic-poetic' words (e.g. *sopire* and *ditare*) which occur throughout the extant books, another set which occurs in the first and then only in the fourth and fifth decades like *grassari* and *interfari*, and yet another list of words like *affatim* and *astu* occurring only after the first eight books. Finally as the *coup de grâce*

---

[1] H. V. Canter, 'Rhetorical Elements in Livy's Direct Speeches', *AJP* xxxviii (1917), 125 ff.; xxxix (1918), 44 ff.; Ullmann, see p. 27 n. 5.

[2] 'Les clausules métriques dans les discours de Salluste, Tite-Live, Tacite', *SO* iii (1925), 65 ff. The double spondee is easily the commonest form, followed by spondee/peon and double choree, then by dactyl/trochee, cretic/trochee, and double cretic.

[3] E. Wölfflin, 'Livianische Kritik und livianischer Sprachgebrauch' (Prog. Winterthur, 1864), 29 ff.; S. G. Stacey, 'Die Entwickelung des livianischen Stiles', *ALL* x (1896), 17 ff.

[4] L. R. Palmer, *The Latin Language* (London, 1954), 137 ff.; E. Löfstedt, *Syntactica* II[2] (Lund, 1942), 294 ff.; E. Burck, *Die Erzählungskunst*[2] (p. 8 n. 2), xxiv.

[5] K. Gries, *Constancy in Livy's Latinity* (New York, 1947).

[6] 'Beobachtungen und Erwägungen zum Wandel der livianischen Sprache', *WS* N.F. ii (1968), 103 ff.

he analyses fr. 60 (the account of the death of Cicero) to demonstrate its highly poetic texture. The conclusion is abundantly clear. Livy continues to use a poetic and archaic diction throughout; and the chief reason for his doing so is that such a diction is traditionally appropriate to *historia*, as the fragments of Coelius Antipater and the works of Sallust show.[1] Of course, the content of a particular book may lend itself to more poetic diction than another, and accordingly there will be statistical variations. But there is no question of Livy's reverting to a classical prose-style.

Tränkle argues, again I think rightly, that too much has been made of the celebrated passage in the elder Seneca[2] in which Livy's hostility to Sallust is asserted. For this is not evidence of stylistic abhorrence, though elsewhere Livy proclaims Demosthenes and Cicero as ideal models,[3] and his own *lactea ubertas* turns away from the studied simplicity of the Sallustian presentation. But Sallust and Livy share a common genre, and there are many parallels in diction and syntax. Tränkle is content to offer one speculative example of Sallustian influence on Livy,[4] but more general resemblances are obvious. For example, the character-sketches of Catiline in Sallust and Hannibal in Livy are strikingly similar.[5] The work of Chausserie-Laprée could be the basis for systematic study and fruitful progress in this area.

So far as formal syntax is concerned, no specialized study of Livian usage has appeared this century, and this poses considerable problems for the student of Livy's Latinity. The monograph of L. Kühnast[6] is a useful exposition of case-usages, and contains valuable information on sundry other matters, but the absence of indexes limits its serviceability as a work of reference. By contrast, O. Riemann's book[7] is well organized and indexed, but deals only with the main headings; it has a useful appendix on the chief differences between Livy's syntax and that of Cicero and Caesar. R. B. Steele analysed Livy's use of the genitive, accusative, and ablative.[8] From Scandinavia, where traditional philology is still pursued, has come a useful study of concessive constructions.[9]

---

[1] Tränkle might have added that some usages are most easily explicable as *borrowings* from Coelius; so *satias* is found three times only, all in the third decade where Livy follows Coelius.

[2] *Contr.* ix. 1. 14: 'T. Livius tam iniquus Sallustio fuit ut hanc ipsam sententiam et tamquam translatam et tamquam corruptam dum transfertur obiceret Sallustio . . .'

[3] See Quint. x. 1. 39.

[4] Sall. *BJ* xx. 2, 'metuens magis quam metuendus'; Livy ii. 12. 8, 'metuendus magis quam metuens'.

[5] Sall. *Cat.* 14–16; Livy xxi. 4.

[6] L. Kühnast, *Die Hauptpunkte des livianischen Syntax* (Berlin, 1872).

[7] O. Riemann, *Études sur la langue et la grammaire de Tite-Live*[2] (Paris, 1885).

[8] R. B. Steele, *Case-usage in Livy: Genitive, Accusative, Ablative* (Leipzig, 1910, 1912, 1913).

[9] E. Mikkola, *Die Konzessivität bei Livius* (Helsinki, 1957).

For many detailed Livian usages the best quarries are the general works, especially Kühner–Stegmann, Hofmann–Szantyr, and (on a more modest scale) S. A. Handford's book on the subjunctive.[1] It is to be hoped that some scholar will attempt the necessary work of synthesis in this area.

On the clausulae in the narrative, it is enough to refer to the systematic discussion of Chausserie-Laprée.[2]

We can close this survey of Livy's Latinity with a brief consideration of Asinius Pollio's charge of *Patavinitas*. Quintilian makes it clear that the sneer was directed at Livy's Latin.[3] Though it has been suggested by one scholar that the reference was to his pronunciation and spelling,[4] it is more probable that the charge was laid against a general provincialism of style.[5] Since Pollio was noted for his spare and jejune Latinity, the censure may well have been directed at the *lactea ubertas* which for Pollio may have evoked the pomposity of Cisalpine worthiness; from here it is only a step further to the suggestion of Syme and others that Pollio was criticizing Livy's 'whole moral and romantic view of history'.[6] But it is worth emphasizing that Quintilian evidently assumed that Pollio was condemning not Livy's historical vision but his Latin.

---

[1] S. A. Handford, *The Latin Subjunctive* (London, 1947).

[2] See p. 26 n. 1, 419 ff.   [3] Quint. i. 5. 56, viii. 1. 3.

[4] J. Whatmough, 'Quemadmodum Pollio reprehendit in Livio Patavinitatem', *HSCP* xliv (1933), 95 ff.

[5] See K. Latte, 'Livy's *Patavinitas*', *CP* xxxv (1940), 56 ff.

[6] R. Syme, *The Roman Revolution*, 485; cf. McDonald (p. 23 n. 3), 72, and Mazza (p. 7 n. 1), 72 f.

IV. NACHLEBEN[1]

LIVY'S history at once became a classic. During the centuries of empire it was not merely read and quoted,[2] but became the quarry for successive epic poets essaying historical themes.[3] Above all, it was consulted by chroniclers, and after being recommended reading in its own right for students it was studied in more compendious form.[4] Then too the more ambitious historian like Tacitus pays Livy the compliment of artistic imitation.[5]

With the eclipse of the western empire, however, and the advent of a murkier era for Roman culture, the fame of Livy was kept alive only by isolated individuals like Orosius and Cassiodorus. B. Doer's useful essay[6] traces the story of this decline and the ensuing wider diffusion of Livy's work amongst the monasteries and schools of the Carolingian period, when Fridugis of Tours, Lupus of Ferrières, and the obscure Dutch bishop Theatbert of Duurstede initiated renewed interest in Livian studies; neglect again follows, but again there is a modest revival in Livy's fortunes during the eleventh to the thirteenth centuries, measurable by the entries in library catalogues and by quotations in historians. This new revival can be easily traced by consulting the indexes in the volumes of Manitius and De Ghellinck.[7]

But Livy's finest hour comes with the enthusiasm of scholars and antiquaries of the Italian Renaissance. Dante's tribute in Canto 28 of the *Inferno*, 'Livio che non erra' (a tag much loved by those who set examination-papers), may be the respectful judgement of one unimpeded by close acquaintance. But others closely studied and passionately ad-

[1] The surveys in Sandys, Bolgar, and Highet can be complemented by the attractive treatment of C. Giarratano, *Tito Livio*[2] (Rome, 1943), ch. 12. The importance of Livy for Bruni is set out in D. J. Wilcox, *The Development of Florentine Humanist Historiography* (Harvard, 1969), 106 f.

[2] See, for example, Seneca *Ep.* xlvi. 1; Quint. x. 1. 101; Pliny, *Ep.* ii. 3. 8, vi. 20. 5.

[3] Perhaps beginning with Virgil (see A. Rostagni, *Da Livio a Virgilio e da Virgilio a Livio* [Padua, 1942]), the list includes Petronius' *De Bello Civili* (see H. Stubbe, *Die Verseinlagen im Petron* [Leipzig, 1933], 104 ff.), Lucan (see R. Pichon, *Les sources de Lucain* [Paris, 1912]), Silius Italicus (so J. Nicol, *The Historical and Geographical Sources used by Silius Italicus with special reference to Livy* [Oxford, 1936]).

[4] Quint. ii. 5. 18 f. recommends it for school-reading; for the Summaries see above, Chapter IIG.

[5] Tacitus' debts to Livy are noted (with bibliography) in F. R. D. Goodyear's survey of Tacitus in this series (1970), 38; see also Grant (p. 3 n. 5), 292. There is scope for further research here.

[6] B. Doer, 'Livy and the Germans', in *Livy* (p. 3 n. 5), 98 ff.

[7] M. Manitius, *Geschichte der lateinischen Literatur des Mittelalters*, III (Munich, 1931); J. De Ghellinck, *L'essor de la littérature latine au XIIe siècle*[2] (Brussels, 1954).

mired. B. L. Ullman's documentation of the period has been notably extended by the work of G. Billanovich, who has outlined Petrarch's part in uniting for publication in a single manuscript the first, third, and fourth decades, and who in another publication has studied Boccaccio's part in diffusing the work of the historian.[1] Another specialized contribution has come from the pen of Albinia de la Mare, who has traced the later history of Livy manuscripts in fifteenth-century Florence.[2] Doer's chapter already mentioned describes the enthusiastic search by Poggio, Salutati, Niccoli, and others for Livy's lost decades, and carries us into the Reformation period in which Luther read Livy, but 'without admiration'. Particularly striking as a facet of Livy's ubiquitous presence amongst humanists is his authority amongst antiquarian archaeologists like Biondo.[3] But perhaps the most conspicuous influence exercised by Livy is on Machiavelli's political treatises; this has been analysed by J. H. Whitfield, and elsewhere by two other scholars writing in English.[4]

The stream of editions since the invention of printing reveals the extent to which Livy has influenced the intellectual, historical, and political consciousness of Europe. This influence has been greatest in Italy[5] and in France, where the historian has exercised effects not merely on academic political theorists but on those who precipitated the Revolution.[6] His influence in the mainstream of British intellectual life has been less pronounced.[7] There is room for a comprehensive study of Livy's influence in Europe since the Renaissance.

[1] B. L. Ullman, *Studies in the Italian Renaissance* (Rome, 1955), ch. 4; G. Billanovich, 'Petrarch and the Textual Tradition of Livy', *Journal of the Warburg and Courtauld Institutes* xiv (1951), 137 ff.; 'Il Boccaccio, il Petrarca, et le più antiche traduzioni in italiano di Tito Livio', *Giorn. stor. lett. ital.* cxxx (1953), 311 ff.

[2] A. de la Mare, 'Florentine Manuscripts of Livy', in *Livy* (p. 3 n. 5), 177 ff.

[3] Texts are given in Valentino–Zucchetti, *Codice tipografico della città di Roma* (Rome, 1946).

[4] J. H. Whitfield, 'Machiavelli's use of Livy', in *Livy* (p. 3 n. 5), ch. 4; cf. C. Roebuck in *Phoenix* vi (1952), 52 ff., and W. S. Anderson in *CJ* liii (1957/8), 232 ff.

[5] C. Giarratano's survey (p. 32 n. 1) is useful here.

[6] It is surprising that there has been no study of Livy's importance for French intellectual and political history. He was Voltaire's favourite historian (see J. H. Brumfitt, *Voltaire, Historian* [Oxford, 1958], 141 f.). His influence on Montesquieu is well traced by Sheila M. Mason, 'Livy and Montesquieu', in *Livy* (p. 3 n. 5), ch. 5. For the influence of Cicero and Livy on the French Revolution see H. T. Parker, *The Cult of Antiquity and the French Revolutionaries* (Chicago, 1937).

[7] M. L. Clarke's *Classical Education in Britain 1500–1900* (Cambridge, 1959) attests his continuing presence in university and school curricula, but few major literary figures reflect a formative influence. An exception is Macaulay; see K. R. Prowse, 'Livy and Macaulay', in *Livy* (p. 3 n. 5), ch. 6.

V. CONCLUSION

WHEN we salute a historian as master of his craft, we recognize in him a combination of four outstanding qualities. First, he has made himself thoroughly cognizant of all the evidence, written or otherwise, with which to interpret his period, and he has the skill to evaluate it. Secondly, he possesses the imaginative insight to transmute this evidence into a living experience of the society he describes, so that the reader can enter into the conditions of life and understand the psychology of the people of the time. Thirdly, he has the intellectual capacity to recognize historical patterns of evolution or change, to relate individual incidents and individual careers to this process of historical development; thus historiography becomes more than the description of a series of static situations, for the historian becomes the moving camera which fuses them. Finally, our ideal historian will have the requisite literary talent to channel his skills with clarity and strength, so as to imprint his interpretation indelibly on the reader's mind.

These four qualities—skill in research, imaginative insight, genius in historical interpretation, literary artistry—are rarely discerned in the same man. Of the ancient historians, Tacitus approximates most closely to the ideal. For Livy we can certainly claim the faculties of imaginative insight and literary skill, but Tacitus is much superior as researcher and as original interpreter. Of course, Tacitus' chosen themes of the Flavian and Julio-Claudian eras were less demanding than Livy's broader subject of the history of Rome *ab initio;* of course, the absence of Livy's version of events after the fall of Carthage makes any close comparison unprofitable. Yet the proximity of Tacitus clarifies the two major defects of Livy. First, he has less talent for the collection and critical evaluation of the evidence; he is painstaking, and often assembles a more comprehensive range of facts than does Tacitus, but this very virtue is germane to the second deficiency. Tacitus' more selective sifting of the source-material reflects the discrimination of the superior interpreter. What we miss in Livy is precisely the shaping control which allows Tacitus to create the pattern of interpretation which Edward Gibbon so much admired.[1]

Livy's defects as researcher and interpreter are partly explicable by the canons of *historia* to which he subscribed. He is not primarily interested in the minutiae of exact research, nor again in the evolution of impersonal historical processes. For Livy, history is the battle-

[1] See Harold Bond, *The Literary Art of Edward Gibbon* (Oxford, 1960).

field of manners. It provides lessons for community and personal living. In this vision of history, the two other attributes—the imaginative vision to relive the experiences of the past, and the literary talent to imprint them on the reader's mind—are overwhelmingly more important. In the convergence of these two qualities, his psychological insight and the literary talent admired by so many from Tacitus to Housman,[1] Livy's genius resides.

---

[1] Housman's admiration for Livy as the greatest of Latin prose-stylists is unfortunately not documented, but the statement in L. P. Wilkinson's *Golden Latin Artistry* (p. 26 n. 2), 187, rests on reliable oral testimony.

APPENDIX

INSTRUMENTA[1]

A. *The Text*

Editions The most important contributions to the establishment of the text have been:

1 Io. Andreas Bussi (*editio princeps*)   Rome, 1469 (?)
Contains only I–X, XXI–XXXII, XXXIV–XL. 37. 3; the sole manuscript of the fifth decade was not rediscovered till the sixteenth century.

2 Carbach   Mainz, 1519

3 Beatus Rhenanus Gelenius   Basle, 1535
(*ed. Frobeniana altera;* includes XLI–XLV)

4 J. F. Gronow (= Gronovius)   Leiden, 1645

5 Crevier   Paris, 1735–42

6 Drakenborch   Leiden, 1738–46

7 Alschefski (I–X, XXI–XXII)   Berlin, 1841–6

8 Weissenborn   (Teubner) Leipzig, 1851
Re-edited by Müller–Heraeus, 1887–1908. A revised Teubner edition of XXI–XXII has been published (1971) by Dorey.

9 Madvig–Ussing   Copenhagen, 1861–6

10 Conway–Walter–Johnson–McDonald   Oxford, 1914–65
I–XXXV thus far; it provides the only full apparatus criticus. I–V has been revised by Ogilvie (?1974). Work on the final volumes (XXXVI–XL, XLI–XLV and fragments) continues.

11 Bayet–Jal   (Budé) Paris, 1940–71
I–VII (Bayet), XLI–XLII (Jal) thus far.

Opuscula

1 Lorenzo Valla, *Emendationes sex librorum T. Livi*   1446–7
Books XXI–XXVI

2 Walch, *Emendationes Livianae*   Berlin, 1815

3 Madvig, *Emendationes Livianae*   Copenhagen, 1860

---

[1] Of particular importance for Livian texts and commentaries of the Renaissance is the survey of A. H. McDonald, *Catalogus Translationum et Commentariorum: Mediaeval and Renaissance Latin Translations and Commentaries.* Volume II: Livius, Titus (Washington, D.C., 1971).

4 Harant, *Emendationes et adnotationes ad T. Livium*   Paris, 1880

5 Luchs, *Emendationum Livianarum particula prima–tertia*
                                                     Erlangen, 1881–7

B. *Commentaries*

1 The first known is by the Dominican Nicholas Trevet; see Ruth M. Dean, 'The earliest known Commentary on Livy', *Med. et Hum.* ii (1945), 86 ff.   1318

2 Glareanus, *Annotationes*   Basle, 1540

3 Sigonius, *Scholia*   Venice, 1555

4 Modius   Frankfurt, 1588

5 Ruperti, *Commentarius perpetuus in T. Livii Patavini Historiarum libros*
                                                      London, 1835
Contains useful historical and linguistic annotation.

6 Weissenborn–Müller   Berlin, 1860–4; 2nd ed. 1880
Regularly reprinted to 1962. It is difficult to imagine this prodigious work of scholarship's being supplanted. The editors have a fine eye for Livian usage; they provide a good text and good linguistic annotation, though they are naturally less informative and often outdated on the historical content.

7 R. M. Ogilvie, *Commentary on Livy Books I–V*   Oxford, 1965
Not a philological commentary on the systematic scale of Weissenborn–Müller, but a more selective series of discussions on the historical, legal, literary, and textual problems, with useful bibliographies appended.

8 Briscoe, *Historical Commentary on Livy XXXI–XXXIII*   Oxford, 1973
Became available after I had completed this survey, but a rapid scrutiny suggests that it provides assistance similar to that offered by Ogilvie's book; Walbank's *Commentary on Polybius* has, however, made detailed bibliographies unnecessary.

9 Amongst the numerous editions of individual books the following are noteworthy:

I	Edwards	Cambridge, 1912
	Heurgon	Paris, 1963
II	Conway	Cambridge, 1901
V	Whibley	Cambridge, 1890
IX	Anderson	Cambridge, 1909
XXI–XXII	Riemann–Benoist	Paris, 1881
XXI	Dimsdale	Cambridge, 1894
XXII	Vallet	Paris, 1966
	Dimsdale	Cambridge, 1893
XXIII–XXIV	Macaulay	London, 1885
XXVII	Campbell	Cambridge, 1913
XXX	Butler–Scullard	London, 1939

C. *Translations*

Livy has played an important part in the cultural history of Europe largely through influential translations. The most celebrated of these are:

French	Bersuire	1352
Spanish	Lopez de Ayala	1407
Italian	Nardi	1540
	(preceded by a considerable number of earlier versions, including Boccaccio's)	
German	Schöfferlin–Wittig	1505
English	Philemon Holland	1600
Scots	Bellenden	1533
	(Books I–V only; edited 1822)	

Of more recent translations in English, the Loeb edition (Foster–Sage–Schlesinger, 1919–59) deserves high praise. Inevitably there are errors, but in general the volumes combine reliability with useful historical annotation and good maps. The final volume, containing the Summaries and Fragments, has a comprehensive Index by Geer which is very useful.

De Selincourt's translation of the first and third decades (London, 1960–5) is composed in supple and vigorous English, and is useful especially for those who wish to read independently of the Latin.

D. *Lexica*

Fügner's *Lexicon* (Leipzig, 1897), unlike a dozen others projected, at least got off the ground but faded after A–B. Hence it was necessary until recently to rely on Ernesti's *Glossarium Livianum* (Leipzig, 1769, recently reissued). As a tool for Livian research, it was better than nothing, but since it made no attempt to be comprehensive, it could lead scholars into hasty judgements on particular usages.

Now, however, a full Concordance has appeared: David W. Packard, *A Concordance to Livy*, 4 vols. (Cambridge, Mass., 1968). This is arguably the most important ancillary to Livian studies ever published. It was completed by computer within a year, and accordingly has inevitable deficiencies. It does not distinguish between different words with the same visual form; it does not group different parts of the same word under a single heading; it does not classify different usages of the same word; it cannot warn the reader when a reading is the foible of an editor rather than the version offered by the best manuscripts. This is because the concordance reproduces a fixed number of words per line from the O.C.T. (I–XXXV) or the Teubner (XXXVI–XLV). Even so, an aspiring editor, or a scholar examining Livian diction, can now for the first time systematically analyse Livy's usage throughout the extant books. R. M. Ogilvie[1] strikingly shows how the evidence of the Concordance tells against several of the O.C.T. readings in IX. Perhaps I may offer a simple example from xxvi. 13. 11. There the Puteanus has 'transgressus Anienem amnem'; the O.C.T. excises *amnem* with the explanation 'Anio vocatur fluvius solito Latino more'. The Concordance shows that Livy writes *Anienem amnem* twice elsewhere, and *amnem* is accordingly to be retained.

[1] R. M. Ogilvie, 'Notes on Livy IX', *YCS* xxiii (1973), 159 ff.